Will You Hear It?

Savannah Alan

WestBow
PRESS
A DIVISION OF THOMAS NELSON

Scripture taken from the HOLY BIBLE, NEW INTERNATIONAL
VERSION®. Copyright © 1973, 1978, 1984 by International Bible Society.
Used by permission of Zondervan Publishing House. All rights reserved.

The "NIV" and "New International Version" trademarks are registered in the
United States Patent and Trademark Office by International Bible Society. Use
of either trademark requires the permission of International Bible Society.

WestBow Press books may be ordered through booksellers or by contacting:

WestBow Press
A Division of Thomas Nelson
1663 Liberty Drive
Bloomington, IN 47403
www.westbowpress.com
1 (866) 928-1240

Because of the dynamic nature of the Internet, any web addresses or
links contained in this book may have changed since publication and
may no longer be valid. The views expressed in this work are solely those
of the author and do not necessarily reflect the views of the publisher,
and the publisher hereby disclaims any responsibility for them.

Any people depicted in stock imagery provided by Thinkstock are
models, and such images are being used for illustrative purposes only.
Certain stock imagery © Thinkstock.

ISBN: 978-1-4908-1494-0 (sc)
ISBN: 978-1-4908-1493-3 (e)

Library of Congress Control Number: 2013920428

Printed in the United States of America.

WestBow Press rev. date: 11/19/2013

Contents

Section One

Introduction

Are you one of those people who don't believe that God still speaks to man? I mean directly to an individual, one on one, and tells them to do something specific. You may entertain the idea that it *"might"* have been possible that He spoke to Moses or Noah or one of the great prophets of old, but for someone in today's realm of society to actually claim that God spoke to them directly is not only far-fetched but seriously verging on the edge of insanity. Right?

Well, if that's the mindset you have then I challenge you to continue reading. And after you have finished if you are still convinced that God doesn't speak to individuals to give them specific commands then you are welcome to call me a liar. You can call me up, send me an email or text (I know, I'm old school), or better yet just come tell me face to face. It's okay. I totally understand how you can find it hard to believe God would do that because I found it hard to believe, even when it happened to me. Oh I believe God still speaks to people. I just found it very hard to believe He would speak so directly to me. I mean, why would He?

Savannah Alan

Nevertheless, He did speak to me. And let me tell you, when God speaks directly to you and tells you to do something, you have only two choices. Either you obey Him, or you spend the rest of your life being absolutely miserable.

It's as if He has placed something inside of you. Something alive and constantly struggling to get out. You can't simply ignore it in hopes that it will go away, because the more you try to suppress it, the harder it will fight to get out. It has a distinct purpose, and in order to fulfill that purpose, it has to be set free. But the only way to set it free, and yourself along with it, is to obey God and share it with those who He wants to receive it.

I pray God will prepare your hearts and minds to receive this exactly as He intends.

The Call

IN THE BEGINNING... -no that's been done.

ONCE UPON A TIME... -uh, don't think so.

God, you told me to share this but how do I do it? I mean, I still find it hard to believe myself. How on earth am I going to tell others in a way that they will believe it? Yes, You're right. I have to leave that up to You. Okay, here we go, Lord. Please take this in the direction *You* want it to go. I want only to share what *You* have given me. Nothing more. Nothing less.

I suppose this all started when I felt a burden for my family and an urgency for them to be reminded of what God has promised will certainly come to pass one day. I could see some of them slipping away from the foundation of truth that God is our only hope for salvation. He is the only stability we have in this rapidly deteriorating world we live in. And if we choose to exclude Him from our lives, intentionally or unintentionally, there will be a great price to pay for that horrible mistake.

As a Christian family, we have been taught that one day Jesus will come and take the children of God home to live with Him throughout all eternity. But we have also been taught that if we stray from God and do not obey Him, a drastically different eternity awaits us. A time of great tribulation and the cursed eternity that is portrayed in the book of Revelation.

The book of Revelation is not easily digested by many people. Personally, I find it intriguing so I have read it numerous times. Yes, it's scary. And yes, it can be confusing. But when you ask God to help you understand it, you will gain amazing insight. You will come to realize that God is and always will be in control. Knowing and accepting that, my friend, is where you find true peace.

I want my family and friends to know that peace, so I felt led to put together a small booklet to attempt to summarize the book of Revelation as simply as possible. I printed it out and gave it to those I felt led to give it to, thinking, *"Okay, I did what God wanted me to do. They can accept it for what it is or ridicule me for doing it. But it's done."*

But it wasn't done. God wasn't finished with me. There was more for me to do.

I firmly believe that God puts us in specific places and shows us specific things for a reason. God has placed me in a job that sometimes allows me to see and hear things I would rather not.

One particular day, I found myself being introduced to some classified information I immediately recognized as something that had been clearly prophesied in the Bible. Now, of course, I can't reveal what I saw because I would lose my job. So as with all things I come across of that nature, I tried to pass it off as just another one of those things I don't want to know about. But this was something I couldn't put out of my mind. Over the next few days and then weeks, I just couldn't get away from it. I pondered over it and thought, *"What am I supposed to do with this? I can't tell anyone about it so I need to just forget about it."* But that wouldn't happen. I started praying for guidance as to what God wanted me to get from this. Was He trying to show me something? Did He want me to react to it in some way? What?

I finally realized that God must be using it to spark an interest in me to dig a little deeper. Not deeper into classified information I don't have any business seeing but deeper into what is actually going on in the world around me that I try so hard to ignore. I don't even watch the news because, quite frankly, the average person can't tell what's real anyway. The government only tells the media what it wants to report, and believe me, it has no problem whatsoever with telling a bold-faced lie.

But still, I felt that God was trying to show me something. Something I would need to share with others. When I finally accepted that, I knew I would need a lot of help to be able to understand what God wanted me to see and share. I felt that I needed to seriously pray and fast for wisdom, guidance, and discernment. Then I started researching information that I might be able to share by writing another booklet for my family and maybe a few friends.

But oh my! Once I started researching, I found far more than I had bargained for. I thought, *"God, this is some heavy stuff! What am I supposed to do with this?"* Feeling that I was about to go into information overload, I turned to God's Word for comfort and guidance. I read a couple of chapters in the Bible but still felt unsettled. I decided I would read some more, but first - I stopped and prayed, *"God, please show me what You want me to do with these things You are obviously bringing to my attention. Help me to clearly understand and do what You want me to do with them."*

I picked up my Bible and starting reading again. I was in the book of Ezekiel and had come to the thirty third chapter. Now let me just say, I have read the Bible from cover to cover more times than I can remember, and it still amazes me how it never gets old. That's because each time I read it, there is always, always something I didn't catch the time before. You know how when you watch a good movie for the second time and you see something really cool and say, "Hey, I missed that the last time"? Well, that's how it is with God's Word, and I believe there is a reason for that. I truly believe that God points out things to you at exactly the right time for you to use them.

I know God guides us with His Word. Many times I have read something and immediately knew, *"Yep, that was for me."* I love it when that happens! Okay, so here I am, reading Ezekiel 33:1-6, which says,

> *The word of the LORD came to me: "Son of man, speak to your countrymen and say to them: 'When I bring the sword against a land, and the people of the land choose one of their men and make him their watchman, and he sees the sword coming against the land and blows the trumpet to warn the people, then if anyone hears the trumpet but does not take warning and the sword comes and takes his life, his blood will be on his own head. Since he heard the sound of the trumpet but did not take warning, his blood will be on his own head. If he had taken warning, he would have saved himself. But if the watchman sees the sword coming and does not blow the trumpet to warn the people and the sword comes and takes the life of one of them, that man will be taken away because of his sin, but I will hold the watchmen accountable for his blood."* (NIV)

What is that supposed to mean? I wasn't just feeling that God was nudging me. I had specifically asked Him to "show me" what He wanted me to do with the information. I sincerely wanted to know what I was supposed to do with it. But this stopped me in my tracks! I closed my Bible and was like- "What?" I read the verses several more times and then said, "Wait a minute. --God, did You just tell me? --nah, couldn't be. But-- surely You are not calling me to be a watchman.

9

Are You asking me to warn my countrymen, family, and friends about something?" I told myself I was being ridiculous because there was no way this could have been intended for me. I mean, good grief, it clearly says, "Son of man," and I am not a son.

I opened my Bible and began reading again.

> *When I say to the wicked, '"O wicked man, you will surely die,"' and you do not speak out to dissuade him from his ways, that wicked man will die for his sin, and I will hold you accountable for his blood. But if you do warn the wicked man to turn from his ways and he does not do so, he will die for his sin, but you will have saved yourself.* (Ezekiel 33:8–9 NIV)

Yes, I had asked God to show me how to reach my family and friends. I had even asked Him to use me to help draw them closer to Him. But this... Isn't this something that preachers, and pastors, and such are supposed to do? God sets them up as leaders and makes them watchmen to warn people like He used the prophets back in biblical times. They are called for such things and expect to be used in that way.

I wrestled with this for some time. Did God really expect *me* to warn the wicked? But wait. Didn't I ask Him to use me? Didn't I pour out my broken heart to Him and cry out for the salvation of my family and friends? Yes, Lord, I did. But God, people don't listen to things like that anymore. And then He clearly spoke to my heart, saying,

"Some will listen.
And they will be saved."

The Warning

God sends His warning to us as just that. A warning. A message to guide us down the right path. Unfortunately most people do not care to listen. We would rather hear a pleasant message reminding us that God loves us, and we are doing the things we should, so just keep up the good work, and all will be fine. Or, even if things are not going exactly the way we think they should, *we* still have things under control and we don't need His advice just yet. But when God sends us a warning, it's not meant to make us feel good. He is trying to prepare us for something that is definitely coming.

The Bible tells us that God places a hedge of protection around those who are His, and as long as we obey Him, we are protected from evil and destruction. But when people decide that God's way is not particularly the way *they* want to go and they, little by little stray from His will, that hedge of protection will be lifted. God loves us and wants to protect us, so He will send us a wake-up call to warn us that we are in danger. Outside the wall of God's protection is <u>not</u> where we want to be.

But the choice is ours as to whether we acknowledge that warning and take heed, or simply ignore it and think, *"It's okay God, I've got this."* America has received several such warnings in the last few years. Wake-up calls that we chose to ignore. Instead of turning to God for protection we look to national security to fortify our defenses and form strategic alliances. But there is no political or military power that can equal the protection we can receive from the hand of the Almighty God. If we think for one minute that our nation can stand on its own, without the help of the *One upon whom it was founded*, we are in far greater danger than we realize. To think we can survive without turning back to God is a fatal illusion.

God sometimes sends us warnings through those who will listen to Him and care enough to share those warnings with others. God has given me the ability to care enough about *you* to risk being ridiculed in order to warn you that we, as Americans are treading on dangerous ground.

> *"...because your sins are so many and your hostility so great, the prophet is considered a fool, the inspired man a maniac."* (Hosea 9:7 NIV)

Although I may be considered a maniac, I must do what God has commanded me to do. I must be a watchman for my family and friends because I love you and I don't want to be held accountable for not sounding the trumpet of warning.

The Reason

God's greatest means of warning us is through His Word. There is good reason why the Bible has so many books on prophecy. God shows us clearly what will happen to a nation when it turns its back on Him. Israel is the prime example. However, if you look closely, it is easy to compare the way Israel became as they turned away from God to go their own way, with the way America has become today.

Israel was a nation that had been formed by God for His own purpose. He even made a covenant with them that they would become the most blessed of all nations, if they would simply follow His ways. But they broke that covenant by turning away from God, to worship the gods of other nations. Instead of worshiping the one and only true God, the Living God, they turned to idols. False gods that were created by man. Instead of obeying God's commands, they abandoned their standards and exchanged their values for the things the nations around them had introduced to them. Gradually they began to desire the things of the world, rather than the things of God. Eventually, they became outright rebellious and completely threw off the holiness and righteousness that God had placed in them. They chose to turn to sensuality, self-interest and profanity, rather than turning back to the God who protected and prospered them. Finally they foolishly rejected Him completely.

The 7th chapter of Micah speaks of the misery of Israel after they had turned away from God and says,

> *2. The godly have been swept from the land… men lie in wait to shed blood… 3. both hands are skilled in doing evil: the ruler demands gifts, the judge accepts bribes, the powerful dictate what they desire – they all conspire together. 4. The best of them is like a brier, the most upright worse than a thorn hedge… 5. Do not trust a neighbor; put no confidence in a friend. Even with her who lies in your embrace be careful of your words. 6. For a son dishonors his father, a daughter rises up against her mother, a daughter-in-law against her mother-in-law – a man's enemies are the members of his own household.*

Sounds a lot like Modern Day America!

The headlines are filled with reports of people killing their own families. The powerful dictate things to be the way *"they"* want them to be. If you have enough money, or even information they want to be kept secret, you can bribe a judge to lean your way in a court case. We can't trust our neighbors because the way we all move around so often, we don't even know who our neighbors really are. So many today are more drawn to sensuality than spirituality. Profanity and perversion are far more prevalent in today's society than are truth and righteousness. Some who profess to be Christians are forsaking the holy and righteous values God has placed within them.

But still, God is reaching out to us. He longs to have a relationship with each one of us. He wants to protect us from what awaits those who have turned away from Him. Jonah 2:8 says,

"Those who cling to worthless idols forfeit the grace that could be theirs." (NIV)

God wants to pour out His grace upon us and bless us.

"God is a gracious and compassionate God, slow to anger and abounding in love, a God who relents in sending calamity." (Jonah 4:2 NIV)

He is a God of second and third chances, even when we don't deserve it. Micah 6:8 tells us,

"He has showed you, O man, what is good. And what does the Lord require of you? To act justly and to love mercy and to walk humbly with your God."

Is that too much for God to ask of those he blesses so abundantly? Absolutely not!

The Coming Disaster

Unlike Israel, who God promised would one day rise again, America has not been given such a promise. America was made great for a season. Once we have completely removed God from our nation, when we no longer allow His ways to be taught to our people, there will be no more protection. He will do as we have asked and bow out, leaving us to our own demise. The nations we have made alliances with will not be interested in helping us. Our own leaders will desert us. They will tuck their tails and run to whatever country they can buy their way into.

Israel will eventually realize their sin and turn to God once more. The Jews, God's chosen people, will be drawn back to Him. He will bring them back to Israel, and they will celebrate. But nowhere in the Bible does it mention America in the end times. Could it be that once God has pulled His people out, He will finally turn His back on the proud and arrogant America that has rejected Him for so long? While Israel is celebrating and praising God for bringing His people home, and the eyes of the world are focused on them, it may be the perfect opportunity for Islamic terrorists, or some other enemy who hates America, to then turn their full anger against us. With the technology they have developed, America could be totally obliterated with a single command.

It's no secret that Russia has been helping Iran develop nuclear weapons for several years. It is also known that there are Al-Qaeda sleeper cells here in America simply waiting for the signal to attack. These terrorists produce suitcase bombs, right here in our own country, that could explode in major cities and kill a million people in the blink of an eye. There are at least seven known teams of terrorists in the United States already. They are working within mosques and Islamic centers, but there is nothing that is being done to thwart this activity. Federal judges will not issue warrants to law enforcement agents to search a mosque or Islamic center for any reason, since such places are listed as *"houses of worship."* Satan has taken one of our most sacred amendments, supporting the separation of church and state, and is using it against us.

As of May 2013, there are at least 165 known mosques and/or Islamic centers in the United States. I say at least, because those are the only ones I could find listed on the internet. The seven known terrorists teams mentioned above have been identified in the cities of Chicago, New York, Washington D.C., Miami, Houston, Los Angeles and Las Vegas. You can see on the map on the next page that six of those seven cities are located near major waterways.

Intelligence reports indicate that Iran has also been developing an EMP (electromagnetic pulse), designed to be used against America. Some believe this is already in place, and only requires the flip of a switch to be initiated. (Don't discredit the possibility that having something of this magnitude within our atmosphere, may even be what is affecting our weather.) The EMP will be used to stop every form of electricity. Now think about that. We have become so technologically dependent, that in an instant, the entire population of the United States of America could be rendered completely helpless. Forget the fact that we will be personally inconvenienced by having no lights, no refrigeration, no heating or cooling, no way of communicating with our families and no transportation. The trucking industry will come to a complete halt! Meaning the stores where we purchase our food and necessities will no longer be restocked. Radio and television stations will go off the air so we will have no idea how wide spread this is, or how long it will last. Computers will no longer function, meaning city and state government offices will be shut down. There will be a nationwide food shortage within days! The military won't even be able to communicate. Our missile defense systems will fail to function. Planes and trains will crash due to their failing electronic systems. Fire trucks and ambulances will be rendered useless for rescuing people because they require electricity to start. Life support systems in hospitals will shut down. In less than a second, we will be like a ship that is dead in the water.

Now take another look at the map that has the seven major cities marked as terrorist locations. It is believed, these strategically placed organizations intend to detonate their bombs simultaneously. Imagine the impact of seven nuclear bombs exploding all at the same time. Just sit back and think about that for a minute and let it sink in. Even if some of us were to survive the nuclear attack, there would be no way help could get to us. Even if other nations were willing to help, there is no way to know how long it would take them to navigate through the massive destruction. They wouldn't be able to fly into the country because of the EMP. The fact that so much of the devastation is on our coastlines, eliminates the help we could receive by ships. We would be completely cut off from the rest of the world.

Perhaps it's time for us to wake up and realize that if we don't take heed to the warnings God has been sending to us, we are going to be in major trouble. I hope you are not naïve enough to think it's going to get better. In fact, it has the potential for getting much, much worse.

America is a nation that God has blessed because it was founded upon Christian principles. But just as Israel did in times past, we have forsaken those principles we once held so dear. We no longer seek God's guidance for our nation, but instead we have allowed other nations to come in and bring with them their own religions. We have set back and allowed them to resurrect their temples and mosques, and call upon their pagan gods, while our own people have gradually pushed aside the only true God. We have slowly become anesthetized to the rituals and cultures that have been brought into our country, so much that we just accept them as *"simply the way it is."* But God is not pleased with that! His Word clearly states that we shall have no others gods before Him.

We may think just because we don't worship these other gods that we are okay. But not so! We must boldly renounce them. We must not allow ourselves or our children to be subjected to them in any way. For us to be passive with them we are saying to our children, "It's okay to practice other religions." But it's not okay.

> *Do not be yoked together with unbelievers. For what do righteousness and wickedness have in common? Or what fellowship can light have with darkness? What harmony*

is there between Christ and Belial? What does a believer have in common with an unbeliever? What agreement is there between the temple of God and idols? For we are the temple of the living God. As God has said" "I will live with them and walk among them, and I will be their God, and they will be my people." Therefore come out from them and be separate, says the Lord. Touch no unclean thing, and I will receive you." "I will be a Father to you, and you will be my sons and daughters, says the Lord Almighty". Since we have these promises, dear friends, let us purify ourselves from everything that contaminates body and spirit, perfecting holiness out of reverence for God. (2 Corinthians 6:14-18 and 7:1 NIV)

Being intrigued by such things is how one is gradually lured into participation with them. One sure way to stir up the wrath of God is to be negligent of the training of His innocent children. To subject them to evil is like spitting in the face of God. He may be patient with it for a while, but it will not last. God is a very loving God and wants to bless us with good things, but in Micah 5:15 He clearly tells us,

"I will take vengeance in anger and wrath upon the nations that have not obeyed me."

We are all *destined to die, and then face judgment.* I don't know about you, but when my time comes to face up to how I chose to live the life God has given me, I want to be able to stand before Him with a clear conscience. I want to know that I have done all I could do to serve Him and no other. We must develop a sense of purpose and urgency, because whether we want to admit it or not, our days are numbered. As the Psalmist says,

> *"Lord, remind me how brief my time on earth will be. Remind me that my days are numbered, and that my life is fleeing away."* (Psalm 39:4 NLT)

After God's church has been raptured, there may be absolutely no more chance for America. The Bible says there will be people who turn to God during the great tribulation. But America may not be a part of those given that chance.

God's chosen people rejected Him, giving us the opportunity to become heirs of the kingdom. NOW is our opportunity. Romans 11:25 says,

> *"...Israel has experienced a hardening in part until the full number of the Gentiles has come in."*

Don't count on being able to live as you please now, in hopes that you will be able to turn to God after He has raptured His church away. The times of the Gentiles may have already been fulfilled by then.

Seek the Lord while He may be found:
call on Him while He is near.
Let the wicked forsake his way
and the evil man his thoughts.
Let him turn to the Lord, and He will
have mercy on him,
and to our God, for He will freely
pardon. (Isaiah 55:6-7 NIV)

A free pardon from our sins is a gift we should never take for granted. God longs for us to come to Him so He can protect us from the coming disaster. We cannot, must not, put our hopes in our nation's leaders to take care of us. We must listen to God's Word. Clearly, He tells us,

"Not by might nor by power, but by my Spirit," says the
Lord Almighty. (Zechariah 4:6 NIV)

But His Spirit will not always strive with man. This world was not meant to last forever. There will come a day when our Heavenly Father finally says, "That's enough."

America's time for turning to God is now! We may think we have plenty of time left, but God is sending us warnings that say otherwise.

I tell you, now is the time of God's favor, now is the day
of salvation. (2 Corinthians 6:2 NIV)

Section Two

Introduction

Most everyone has plans of what we want for our future. It may be a plan to build a large estate, travel to different parts of the world, maybe to have children, retire wealthy, and so on and so forth. But the truth is, we don't know everything the future holds for us. We do know that much of our future will be determined by the choices we make in life. I believe the single most important choice any of us will ever make, is whether or not to allow God to be a part of the life we live.

The Bible tells us there will come a time when Jesus will come back and rapture his church. Meaning, he will gather all of his children, and take us to heaven to live with him forever. If we are among those who are still living at the time of the rapture, we have God's promise of what will happen, depending on the choice we have made. If we made the choice to allow God to direct our lives, then we are promised we will be taken to heaven to live with him throughout eternity. However, for those who chose to exclude God from their lives, the book of Revelation gives us an actual outline of what the future holds for them.

--and it's not pretty.

For those who neglected to include God in the plans for their future there will be a time the Bible refers to as the Great Tribulation. This is a time when God will make one "final" plea, for those who are left here on earth to come to him. Unfortunately, because nothing else has been successful at getting their attention, there will be horrible things to endure during this time of tribulation.

This section is the original portion I wrote for my family. It is an attempt to break it down, step by step, in an effort to help us better understand what is coming.

NOTE: This writing is in no way an in-depth study of the book of Revelation. However, I do hope that it interests you enough that you will research it for yourself.

The Gamble

*Gamble – take a chance, speculation, bet, long shot, run the
risk, shot in the dark, stab, wager, coincidence, destiny, fluke,
haphazard, heads or tails, odds, throw of the dice, toss-up, cast
lots, play with fire, put eggs in one basket, run the risk, skate
on thin ice, venture, try your hand, tempt fate, go for broke,
go out on a limb, be careless, lay on the line, put in jeopardy*

Beginning in the sixth chapter of the book of Revelation,
the very last book of the Bible, it tells of a scroll with seven
seals. Jesus, who gave His life so that we can be ransomed
from this horrible fate, is the only one worthy of opening the
seven seals. As each seal is opened, there is a great and horrible
event that takes place. As you read about these events, keep
in mind that it may be you or your children trying to survive
these horrible things. But more importantly, keep in mind
that at least for now, you still have the opportunity to make
the right choice.

The 7 Seals:

1st Seal – White Horse = A Ruler bent on conquering

The Lamb (Jesus) opened the first of the seven seals.

> (Revelation 6:2 NIV)
> *I looked, and there before me was a white horse! Its rider held a bow, and he was given a crown, and he rode out as a conqueror bent on conquest.*

It should be very clear to us, this ruler will not be a kind and loving king. This will be a harsh ruler, whose main purpose is to conquer and destroy, at any cost. I believe this ruler will be the one the Bible refers to as the Anti-Christ, who will demand that everyone bow down to worship him. Those who refuse to worship him will be violently tortured, in an attempt to *persuade* them to sacrifice their souls to eternal damnation, by surrendering their lives to him.

2nd Seal – Red Horse = War

The Lamb opened the second seal.

> (Revelation 6:4 NIV)
> *Then another horse came out, a fiery red one. Its rider was given power to take peace from the earth and to make men slay each other. To him was given a large sword.*

Imagine a world with absolutely no peace at all.

During this time of tribulation, God will have removed His Spirit from the world. With the absence of God's Spirit to keep at bay the demonic spirits, they will be running rampant. Their job will be to produce as much evil as they can possibly conjure up. They will place in the minds of men the most horrible schemes imaginable. People will live in constant fear of leaving their homes, because it's very likely they will be killed before they can return. They won't be able to allow their children (referring to those born after the Rapture) to play outside for fear that someone will either steal them or kill them. But now imagine not being able to lie down and sleep at night because you can't even trust your own family members. A person without peace is a tortured soul, capable of unimaginable evil.

When peace is taken from the earth, men will kill without regard for who their victims may be. It will not matter if you are a brother, sister, parent or even one's own child. When a person has absolutely no peace, they become capable of horrible things. Things they would otherwise never even dream of doing.

3rd Seal – Black Horse = Famine
The Lamb opened the third seal.

(Revelation 6:5-6 NIV)
I looked, and there before me was a black horse! Its rider was holding a pair of scales in his hand. (6) Then I heard what sounded like a voice among the four living creatures, saying, "A quart of wheat for a day's wages,

and three quarts of barley for a day's wages, and do not damage the oil and the wine!"

This speaks of a famine so severe that you will not be able to buy food for your family. Even those who have money will not be able to find food to buy. People will be starving to death right before your eyes. The elderly and the weak will have no choice but to simply lie down and die.

Those who have any strength at all will be willing to steal, or even kill, to get food. A desperate person quickly becomes whatever they need to be to get what they need. No matter what the cost. Money. Life. Family. Whatever it takes. They will be eager to do *anything* to survive.

I believe the book of Isaiah describes this type of hunger better than anything else I have read. He put it like this:

"Distressed and hungry, they will roam through the land; when they are famished, they will become enraged and, looking upward, will curse their king and their God. Then they will look toward the earth and see only distress and darkness and fearful gloom, and they will be thrust into utter darkness." (Isaiah 8:21-22 NIV)

And then again:

On the right they will devour, but still be hungry; on the left they will eat, but will not be satisfied. Each will feed on the flesh of his own offspring. (Isaiah 9:20 NIV)

Can you imagine being so hungry you would even consider eating your own child to survive? The act of cannibalism is bad enough in and of itself, but in order to be able to eat your children, you must first be able to kill them.

Most parents would rather die than harm one of their own children. I can't imagine what immense desperation a parent would have to feel in order to be able to actually cause the death of their own child, just so they can survive.

Yes, I would say that is true desperation.

4th Seal – Pale Horse = Death to a quarter of all people on the Earth

The Lamb opened the fourth seal.

(Revelation 6:8 NIV)
I looked and there before me was a pale horse! Its rider was named Death, and Hades was following close behind him. They were given power over a fourth of the earth to kill by sword, famine and plague, and by the wild beasts of the earth.

Imagine, if you can, one fourth of the population of the world being wiped out. It's very likely that at least part of your family will be killed during this time.

The Bible doesn't give a specific amount of time it will take for this to happen. However, it does say that all of these judgments (Seals, Trumpets and Plagues) will be within a seven year period. If they happen in succession, as they are written in the book of Revelation, this 4th Seal Judgment will happen within the first three and a half years. This one judgment could happen in the time span of a year, a month, a week or even in a day.

At that time, human lives will be taken four different ways. Death by a sword, death by famine, death by plague, and death by wild beasts. We don't know if these will come one at a time or if they will all happen simultaneously, but I can't imagine any of those deaths could be a more horrible way to die than any of the other ways mentioned. No matter how each death occurs, you can be sure it will be torturous.

5th Seal –The souls of those who had been killed because of the word of God cry out

(Revelation 6:9-11 NIV)
When the fifth seal was opened, I saw under the altar the souls of those who had been slain because of the word of God and the testimony they had maintained. (10) They called out in a loud voice, "How long, sovereign Lord, holy and true, until you judge the inhabitants of the earth and avenge our blood?" (11) Then each of them was given a white robe, and they were told to wait a little longer, until the number of their fellow servants and brothers who were to be killed as they had been was completed.

Those who are tortured and killed because they choose to worship God instead of Satan, are who this verse refers to. Those who refuse to bow down and worship the Anti-Christ. They will be anxious for God to avenge their deaths, and will cry out to him to deal with those who took part in killing them.

God will indeed give them justice. But there will be more who lose their lives for His name sake before the time of the great tribulation is over, so He gives each of these a robe of white and tells them they must wait a little longer before He destroys the enemy for good.

Being the patient God that He is, He wants to give people a little more time to come to Him before there is no more hope for mankind.

6th Seal – A great earthquake, the sun turns black, the moon turns red as blood and the stars fall to the earth

(Revelation 6:12-17 NIV)

When he opened the sixth seal there was a great earthquake. The sun turned black like sackcloth made of goat hair, the whole moon turned blood red, (13) and the stars in the sky fell to earth, as late figs drop from a fig tree when shaken by a strong wind. (14) The sky receded like a scroll, rolling up, and every mountain and island was removed from its place. (15) Then the kings of the earth, the princes, the generals, the rich, the mighty, and every slave and every free man hid in caves and among the rocks of the mountains.

(16) They called to the mountains and the rocks, "Fall on us and hide us from the face of him who sits on the throne and from the wrath of the Lamb! (17) For the great day of their wrath has come, and who can stand?"

Finally, men will begin to realize this is the righteous wrath of God and his Son, Jesus Christ. The God they rejected, and the gift of salvation they refused to accept. Instead, they chose the pleasures and riches of the world. Now they will see the truth of it all, and how deceptive the love of earthly treasures can be. But it will be too late. The material possessions they worked so hard to obtain over the years will be of no use to them now. They will cry out to the mountains and the rocks to cover them, thinking they can actually hide from the horrible things that will be taking place during that awful time. But there will be no hiding. Those who have rejected God for so long, will suffer the consequences of their actions during this terrible time of tribulation.

7th Seal – Fire is hurled upon the earth with thunder, lightning and an earthquake.
This Seal will usher in the 7 trumpet judgments.

(Revelation 8:1-6 NIV)
When he opened the seventh seal, there was silence in heaven for about half an hour. (2) And I saw the seven angels who stand before God, and to them were given seven trumpets. (3) Another angel, who had a golden censer, came and stood at the altar. He was given much incense to offer, with the prayers of all the saints, on the golden altar before the throne. (4) The smoke of the incense, together with the prayers of the saints, went up before God from the angel's hand. (5) Then the angel took the censer, filled it with fire from the altar, and hurled it on the earth; and there came peals of thunder, rumblings, flashes of lightning and an earthquake. (6)

The 7 angels who had the 7 trumpets prepared to sound them.

HALF AN HOUR OF SILENCE IN HEAVEN!!!

Can you imagine? No angels singing. No praises to God. Nothing. Only silence. You might say this is the ultimate "quiet before the storm."

The designated angels are preparing to sound their trumpets. This can only mean something tremendous is about to happen. There has been thunder and lightning, an earthquake, and fire has been hurled to the earth.

But still, something BIGGER is coming.

The 7 Trumpets:

(Revelation 8:7 NIV)
The first angel sounded his trumpet, and there came hail and fire mixed with blood, and it was hurled down upon the earth. A third of the earth was burned up, a third of the trees were burned up, and all the green grass was burned up.

A hail storm? No, not just a hail storm. Hail and fire. Mixed with blood. And it will be hurled down, meaning it will come with hurricane force. Enough force to burn up an entire one third of the earth and its trees.

All of the green grass will be burned up, which includes the earth's vegetation. No more fruits or vegetables to eat, or even to produce seed for growing more.

(Revelation 8:8-9 NIV)
The second angel sounded his trumpet, and something like a huge mountain, all ablaze was thrown into the sea. A third of the sea turned into blood, (9) a third of the living creatures in the sea died, and a third of the ships were destroyed.

At this time, a third of the sea will be turned to blood, causing a third of all sea life to die, and a third of all ships on the sea to be destroyed. No doubt, some of these will be ships bringing food and necessities, medicines and medical supplies to hungry and hurting people. Many of these ships will be cruise liners, with thousands of vacationers on them. And some will even be our military ships, that serve to protect us. Unfortunately, they will never make it to port. These ships, with their supplies and all their crew members and passengers, will be destroyed at sea as this huge mountain comes crashing down on them. The sinking of the Titanic was mild compared to the devastation that will be caused to these ships. There will be no survivors from this ocean voyage.

(Revelation 8:10-11 NIV)

The third angel sounded his trumpet, and a great star, blazing like a torch, fell from the sky on a third of the rivers and on the springs of water – (11) the name of the star is Wormwood. A third of the waters turned bitter, and many people died from the waters that had become bitter.

Not only is the sea ruined, but now the rivers and streams of water as well. This Wormwood star will ruin a third of the earth's sources of drinking water. And many more people will die.

(Revelation 8:12 NIV)

The fourth angel sounded his trumpet, and a third of the sun was struck, a third of the moon, and a third of the stars, so that a third of them turned dark. A third of the day was without light, and also a third of the night.

The earth will have reached a point where a third of it has been totally destroyed! A third of the sea has turned to blood, so that a third of all sea life and ships have been destroyed. A third of the rivers and springs of water have been ruined by a bitterness that has killed many more people. A third of the daytime and a third of the night is total darkness. We can't even begin to imagine how devastating that will be. It was already hard enough to find food, but after this occurs you can pretty

much forget about it. Even the people who have already sold
their souls to the Anti-Christ will be starving.

(Revelation 9:1-11 NIV)

*The fifth angel sounded his trumpet, and I saw a star
that had fallen from the sky to the earth. The star was
given a key to the shaft of the Abyss. (2) When he
opened the Abyss, smoke rose from it like the smoke from
a gigantic furnace. The sun and sky were darkened by the
smoke from the Abyss. (3) And out of the smoke locusts
came down upon the earth and were given power like
that of scorpions of the earth. (4) They were told not to
harm the grass of the earth or any plant or tree, but only
those people who did not have the seal of God on their
foreheads. (5) They were not given power to kill them,
but only to torture them for 5months. And the agony
they suffered was like that of the sting of a scorpion
when it strikes a man. (6) During those days men will
seek death, but will not find it; they will long to die, but
death will elude them. (7) The locusts looked like horses
prepared for battle. On their heads they wore something
like crowns of gold, and their faces resembled human
faces. (8) Their hair was like women's hair, and their
teeth were like lion's teeth. (9) They had breastplates like
breastplates of iron, and the sound of their wings was like
the thundering of many horses and chariots rushing into
battle. (10) They had tails with stings like scorpions,
and in their tails they had power to torment people for*

five months. (11) They had as king over them the angel of the Abyss, whose name in Hebrew is Abaddon, and in Greek, Apollyon.

LOCUSTS! Millions of locusts!

So many that the sound of their wings will be like the thundering of many horses and chariots rushing into battle. And they have come for only one purpose. To torture!

But these are not your ordinary locusts. These locusts have tails like scorpions! And teeth like a lion's teeth! They are given power to torment people for five long months. They are forbidden to harm what is left of the trees, grass or plants. Their mission is only to torture those who have not been marked with God's seal of protection. Those who are stung by the scorpion tails of these locusts will be in such agony they will cry out for death. But death will not come to them. No, their suffering will not be eased.

(Revelation 9:13-19 NIV)

The sixth angel sounded his trumpet, and I heard a voice coming from the horns of the golden altar that is before God. (14) It said to the sixth angel who had the trumpet, "Release the four angels who are bound at the great river Euphrates." (15) And the four angels who had been kept ready for this very hour and day and month and year were released to kill a third of mankind. (16) The number of the mounted troops was two hundred million. (17) The horses and riders I saw in my vision looked like this: their breastplates were fiery red, dark blue, and yellow as sulfur. The heads of the horses resembled the head of lions, and out of their mouths came fire, smoke and sulfur. (18) A third of mankind was killed by the plagues of fire, smoke and sulfur that came out of their mouths. (19) The power of the horses was in their mouths and in their tails; for their tails were like snakes, having heads with which they inflicted injury.

Just when you thought it couldn't get any worse...

Two hundred million horses and riders are released to kill yet another third of mankind. Did you get that? Two hundred MILLION. Not an army of hundreds, or an army of thousands, or even a few million. No, this is an army of two hundred million.

But still, this is not only an army of warriors on infantry horses. These horses are described as horses with heads like a lion's head, that spew out of their mouths fire, smoke and sulfur. Sounds a lot like modern day battle tanks to me.

And if that's not bad enough, they also have tails like snakes to bite and poison mankind. Keep in mind that when John had this vision, he had no idea what horrible weapons man would come to imagine, and eventually produce in mass quantities.

The poison he speaks of could very well be a glimpse of the chemical weapons used today. Whatever it is, it's lethal. Death and destruction will be everywhere.

But it's not over yet!

(Revelation 12:1-3 NIV)
The seventh angel sounded his trumpet.
A great sign appeared in heaven: a woman clothed with the sun, with the moon under her feet and a crown of twelve stars on her head. (2) She was pregnant and cried out in pain as she was about to give birth. (3) Then another sign appeared in heaven: an enormous red dragon with seven heads and ten horns and seven crowns on his heads. Its tail swept a third of the stars out of the sky and flung them to the earth.

(Revelation 12:7-9 NIV)
Then war broke out in heaven. Michael and his angels fought against the dragon, and the dragon and his angels fought back. (8) But he wasn't strong enough, and they lost their place in heaven. (9) The great dragon was hurled down – that ancient serpent called the devil, or Satan, who leads the whole world astray. He was hurled to the earth, and his angels with him.

(Revelation 12:12 NIV)

"... but woe to the earth and the sea, because the devil has gone down to you! He is filled with fury, because he knows that his time is short."

THE DRAGON! And oh, what a dragon he is. This is no fairytale dragon. This dragon is Satan himself. And boy is he mad! He and his army just lost a major battle and have been hurled to the earth. He is filled with fury. And who do you think he's going to take it out on? All those people who were left behind when that despicable Jesus came down and swooped all of the good saints away.

He knows he has only a short time until he is conquered completely, so he is going to wreak as much havoc on mankind as possible, while he still has the opportunity. The evil we have seen on this earth in our lifetime is nothing compared to the evil that will engulf this world during the last days of Satan's reign.

This event will also wipe out another third of the heavenly lights (stars) causing this world to become an even darker place in which to exist. The world will be in unimaginable chaos. Evil chaos!

(Revelation 13:1-4 NIV)

And the dragon stood on the shore of the sea. And I saw a beast coming out of the sea. He had ten horns and seven heads, with ten crowns on his horns, and on each head a blasphemous name. (2) The beast I saw resembled a leopard, but had feet like those of a bear and a mouth like that of a lion. (3) One of the heads of the beast seemed to have been wounded and had been healed. The whole world was astonished and followed the beast. (4) Men worshiped the dragon who had given authority to the beast and also worshiped the beast and asked, "Who is like the beast? Who can make war against him?"

(Revelation 13:7) *It was given power to wage war against God's holy people and to conquer them. And he was given authority over every tribe, people, language and nation. (8) All inhabitants of the earth will worship the beast – all whose names have not been written in the book of life belonging to the Lamb that was slain.*

Satan will now raise a beast that has the power to deceive what is left of mankind. Many Bible scholars interpret this beast with the ten horns as 10 kings or divisions of power. They will be chosen by Satan to rule for a very short time. They will almost immediately surrender the power they have been given over their kingdoms to the Anti-Christ, making him the supreme ruler over all nations.

Men will worship Satan and his beast and they will wage a mighty war against those who have chosen to follow God, and to conquer them. All the inhabitants of the earth will fall down and worship this beast, except those who have surrendered to God. Those whose names are written in the Lamb's Book of Life.

(Revelation 13:11 NIV)
Then I saw another beast, coming out of the earth. He had two horns like a lamb, but he spoke like a dragon.

(Revelation 13:13-18 NIV) *He performed great and miraculous signs, even causing fire to come down from heaven to earth in full view of men. (14) Because of the great signs he was given power to do on behalf of the first beast, he deceived the inhabitants of the earth. He ordered them to set up an image in honor of the first beast who was wounded by the sword and yet lived. (15) He was given power to give breath to the image of the first beast, so that it could speak and cause all who refused to worship the image to be killed. (16) He also forced everyone, small and great, rich and poor, free and slave, to receive a mark on his right hand or on his forehead, (17) so that no one could buy or sell unless he had the mark, (18) which is the name of the beast, for it is man's number. His number is 666.*

(Revelation 14:9-11 NIV)
If anyone worships the beast and his image and receives his mark on his forehead or the hand, (10) he will be tormented with burning sulfur in the presence of the holy

angels and of the Lamb. (11) And the smoke of their torment rises for ever and ever. There is no rest day or night for those who worship the beast and his image, or for anyone who receives the mark of his name.

Yet another beast will rise. One who will be allowed to perform miraculous signs to further deceive mankind. In his deception, he will order the people to erect an image in honor of the first beast. And he will actually breathe life into the image. Everyone will be forced to worship the image that will come to life, or they will be killed. It will be mandatory for everyone to receive his mark on their hand or forehead. And his mark will be the number 666.

The infamous Mark of the Beast. This horrible mark will be required on everyone. For a time, people may think this is optional, but those who refuse to accept it will not be able to buy or sell anything to survive. Then as time goes on, people will actually be killed for not obeying the law that will be issued, requiring people to take this mark. Not only by those in authority, but by anyone who has a weapon. They will believe they are doing the right thing. John 16:2 tells us,

"a time is coming when anyone who kills you will think he is offering a service to God."

Unfortunately, taking this mark dooms your soul forever. There will be no more hope of salvation for those who succumb to this act of blatant rebellion against the Almighty God. Those who accept the mark of the beast will be tormented with burning sulfur, and the smoke of their torment will rise forever and ever.

Your only hope will be to desperately reach out to God for strength to resist the temptation to receive this mark of eternal damnation.

The 7 Plagues:

(Revelation 15:1 NIV)
I saw in heaven another great and marvelous sign; seven angels with the seven last plagues – last, because with them God's wrath is completed.

(Revelation 16:1 NIV)
Then I heard a loud voice from the temple saying to the seven angels, "Go, pour out the seven bowls of God's wrath on the earth."

This is God's final wrath upon those who refuse to follow Him. Those who time after time, make the choice to ignore Him. To reject Him. God will offer, for the last time, his gift of salvation. Yet, there will still be those who blatantly refuse Him. So the seven angels with the seven last plagues will be told to "Go, pour out the seven bowls of God's wrath on the earth."

1. Ugly, painful sores –

(Revelation 16:2 NIV)

The first angel went and poured out his bowl on the land, and ugly and painful sores broke out on the people who had the mark of the beast and worshiped his image.

Those who have surrendered to Satan and have accepted his mark upon them will now be struck with the first of the seven plagues. Their bodies will break out with not just some itchy rash, but with ugly and painful sores. I can image these being the kind of sores that simply will not heal. The kind of sores that continue to get worse as they become infected, and cause intense pain to your entire body, as your skin begins to literally rot.

2. Sea turns to blood –

(Revelation 16:3 NIV)

The second angel poured his bowl out on the sea, and it turned to blood like that of a dead man, and every living thing in the sea died.

The sea is now nothing but blood, with dead fish floating on it. No more seafood. No more swimming. No more boating. No more going to the beach. (Not that anyone will ever be at leisure to think about a vacation anymore.) But can you imagine the stench? No one will be able to live anywhere near the water. The smell of blood, mixed with dead and rotting sea creatures. It will be so horrible you won't be able to breathe the air. Imagine the disease this is going to cause! Especially for those people whose bodies are already covered in those horrible sores.

3. Rivers and springs turn to blood –

(Revelation 16:4 NIV)
The third angel poured out his bowl on the rivers and springs of water, and they became blood.

No longer just the seas, but now the rivers and the springs of water will have turned to blood as well. That means no water to drink. Don't bother rushing to the store to buy bottled water. Even if you have the mark of the beast so you can purchase things at the store, and even if you have money, or whatever it is the governing powers are forcing you to use for purchasing during this time, think about it. If God has sent a plague to turn the seas, rivers and springs of water to blood, don't you think he will have covered all the water sources?

No, there will be no clean water. ANYWHERE.

4. The sun was given power to scorch people with fire –

(Revelation 16:8 NIV)
The fourth angel poured out his bowl on the sun, and the sun was given power to scorch people with fire and they were seared by the intense heat.

So now you can't even go outside in the daytime, because the heat from the sun is so intense it will literally set you on fire. And if it gets that hot in the daytime, you can be sure it will not be much cooler at night.

People are living in fear. They are starving. Their bodies are racked with pain from the ugly sores all over them. They have no water to drink, or even to wash their sores. And now they have this intense heat to deal with.

What misery! Yet people still refuse to turn to the only One who can help them. In their stubborn rejection of Him, they still refuse to seek God.

5. Plunged into darkness –

(Revelation 16:10 NIV)
The fifth angel poured out his bowl on the throne of the beast, and his kingdom was plunged into darkness. Men gnawed their tongues in agony.

No doubt, the Anti-Christ and his beast will enjoy watching all the people suffering through the torment they must endure during the tribulation. But surely he must realize that God is coming after him now. The throne he has set up for himself has been plunged into utter darkness. His own people will be gnawing their tongues in sheer agony. They must know by now that he cannot do anything to help them. In fact, they will probably now realize he is the reason for all of the suffering, and will begin to turn on him. But it will be too late. They will have already pledged their souls to him. They will suffer the same fate that he will. They will have made their choice. The wrong choice.

6. Euphrates River dries up –

(Revelation 16:12 NIV)
The sixth angel poured out his bowl on the great River Euphrates, and its water dried up to prepare the way for the kings from the East.

This event has already begun to happen. On March 13, 2013 there was an article posted on the Internet announcing the Tigris and Euphrates rivers are losing water reserves at a rapid pace. I strongly urge you to look this up. Posted in the article are satellite images that clearly show an amazing progression in the reduction of the size of the Euphrates River. This is in preparation for those who the Bible refers to as "the kings of the East." There is strong indication that these kings of the East are identified as being from the country of China.

Already there is a road, referred to as an "all-weather road" that has been completed from China to Afghanistan. News reports suggest that China is being armed with WMDs (weapons of mass destruction), consisting of nuclear, chemical and biological weapons that will enable them to wipe out 33% of their enemies, or one third of the world.

Oh, and by the way. Just in case you didn't know, China already has an army of two hundred million men who are ready and willing to go to war for their country. These men have been conditioned since childhood to prepare for this mighty war. Theirs is a culture that is proud to produce male children to be trained for war. So much so that it is believed they secretly kill the female babies, so they can have another chance to give birth to a male child. With great pride, they raise the child to honor his family by giving his life over to the government to be used for fighting. Producing warriors is an act they take very seriously.

7. Lightning, rumblings, peals of thunder and a severe earthquake –

(Revelation 16:17-18 NIV)
The seventh angel poured out his bowl into the air, and out of the temple came a loud voice from the throne,

saying, "It is done!" (18) Then there came flashes of lightning, rumblings, peals of thunder and a severe earthquake. No earthquake like it has ever occurred since man has been on earth, so tremendous was the quake.

An earthquake, like no other earthquake before it. The literal end of the world, as we know it. You may have seen movies depicting the end of the world as some horrific scene, where the earth is shaking and everything is crashing down upon itself, and people are screaming, and death and destruction are everywhere. But then all the actors get to go home, and all is right with the world again. Not this time. Whether you believe in God or not, when He says, "It is done!" …it's really done.

So there you have it. The words you have read here are not from a book of fiction, but straight from the Holy Bible. Warnings from God Himself. Not because he wants to submit anyone to the awful hazards that come from disobeying him, but because he loves us and wants to prevent us from being subjected to these horrible events. However, He will not force us to choose one way over the other. He has given us free will to choose the way we want to live. Now that you have heard the warning, it's a conscious decision on your part. You either choose to follow God and enjoy eternal life with him, or you choose to ignore Him at your own peril. It's not just a roll of the dice or a spin of the wheel this time. Lady Luck has nothing to do with this. The choice is yours! I pray with all my heart that you will make the right one.

He who testifies to these things says,
"Yes, I am coming soon."

Amen. Come, Lord Jesus.

(Revelation 22:20 NIV)

The Good News

So as not to leave you with a helpless and hopeless feeling, I have to tell you... it ain't over yet. Yes, the proverbial "fat lady" is warming up, but she hasn't begun to sing just yet. You can still make the right choice. God loves you! Believe it or not, He wants to have a relationship with you. He is calling you even now to come to Him. He longs to have you join His family and be a part of something wonderful. We can't even imagine the amazing things He has in store for us.

"No eye has seen, no hear has heard, no mind has conceived what God has prepared for those who love Him"
1 Corinthians 2:9

One of the best things about God is that He is always available. No matter what time of the day or night it happens to be where you are, you can have constant access to Him. Becoming a Christian opens up a life of amazing privileges. Through your faith in Jesus Christ, you are transformed into a new creation. You will think differently. You can gain a sense of confidence no one can achieve without the knowledge that

God is directing your steps. He will bathe you in peace that surpasses all understanding, and give you a life far better than any you could have ever imagined for yourself.

How do you do this? Well, my friend, that is the easiest part. When you give your life to Him, He will wipe away your past, no questions asked. He will cleanse you and give you everything you will ever need to live for Him on this earth, and then to live with Him throughout eternity.

All you need to do is sincerely invite Him into your life. Confess to Him that you know you have sinned (which we all have done) and ask Him to forgive you. Accept Jesus into your heart as your Lord and Savior, and you will be a new creature in Christ. It's as easy as that.

You may think you have to change your life before God will accept you as His child, but that's just not true. In fact, you are incapable of changing yourself and making it stick. Only God can change you, and He will do it from the inside out. He will start with your heart and then transform your entire life. Once you give yourself completely to Him then He will make everything new. Of course, the devil will do his best to try to make you think you are no different than before, and he will start showing you things you've done in the past that make you feel as though you are not anyone God could ever want. But he is a liar. Nothing you have ever done is too big for God to forgive. No matter how much you think you have messed up, God can still turn it around and use it for good. Always remember, God is far more powerful than Satan, and He will protect you from anything the devil can throw at you.

As a new Christian, it is very important for you to get plugged into a local church. You need to have the prayer backing of a church, and the support system of Christian friends who will help guide you on your Christian walk. God will use them to bring you strength and encouragement in times when you will need them. And as God touches you, He will use you to touch others.

Being a Christian is not always easy, but it's an amazing experience you will never regret. But here again, it's your choice. You have to decide whether or not you are going to allow God to be a part of your life. Below is a small list of adjectives you may want to consider when making the choice.

J – JOYFUL	S – STAINED
E – ENCOURAGED	A = ALONE
S – SAFE	T – TORMENTED
U – UNAFRAID	A – ABANDONED
S – SUCCESSFUL	N - NOTHING

Section Three

Introduction

Of course, you will want your Christian walk to be a successful one. To achieve success in something most often requires putting at least some level of effort into it. Rarely is anything such as this simply 'given' or 'pronounced upon' you without some degree of effort on your part. The same thing holds true for spiritual success. If you want to attain success, there are some things you will need to work at, in order to get the results you want.

In order to achieve success, you must first be able to define what success is to you as an individual. Your perception of success may be totally different from something someone else may consider to be a success. I'm reminded of when my daughter was in kindergarten. She was a very bright child who was never at a loss for words. So much so that when she would come home from school each day I would immediately look on her daily report to see if she had gotten into trouble for talking when she should have been being quiet. I considered a daily report with no bad marks on it was a successful day. However, her perception of success was to see her name written on the classroom board. With check marks beside it!

Of course, we are speaking of a much higher degree of success than a kindergarten daily report, but it still holds true that success of any type will be an individual perception. To achieve any level of success, there will be certain steps you must take.

> *Not that I have already obtained all this, or have already been made perfect, but I press on to take hold of that for which Christ Jesus took hold of me.* (Philippians 3:12 NIV)

The Stepping Stones to Success

Step 1: Commitment to the plan

Commitment - a willingness to give your time and energy to something that you believe in, or a promise or firm decision to do something; a pledge or promise; to obligate yourself

To achieve a level of success you must first have a plan, and then you must be committed to that plan. If spiritual success is something you seek to obtain then your commitment must be to first learn what God desires from you, and then be completely committed to fulfilling that for Him. Being committed to something takes discipline and sometimes great sacrifice, but being committed to doing God's will also comes with lots of perks.

First of all, we are already given the promise that we will succeed.

> *"Commit to the Lord whatever you do, and your plans will succeed."* (Proverbs 16:3 NIV)

That's not to say that everything will always go the way we want it to go, but as long as we commit to the Lord whatever we do, then we 'will' be successful at it.

We also have the promise that He will never leave us or forsake us. He is going to be right there with us every step of the way. He will provide all the guidance and abilities we need to do everything that needs to be done.

However, we do have to get our priorities in order. In fact, it's all about priorities. Priority number one is to

> **"Seek first the kingdom of God and His righteousness, and all these things will be added to you."** (Matthew 6:33 NIV)

Our relationship with God and doing His will should come before EVERYTHING else. As long as we put God first, there is no way we can go wrong. Even when the situation looks hopeless, if we keep our eyes on God, and stay committed to the task, He will make everything work out for the best.

Jesus gave us the ultimate example of commitment in Matthew 26:39. He was facing death upon a cross, yet still He said,

> **"Not my will, but yours be done."**

We have to remember, God has a purpose for everything. We have to be willing to submit to His perfect will for the plan to come out perfectly.

In order to succeed, your commitment cannot be half-hearted. You must surrender all. God wants us to have so much trust in Him that we are willing to commit to His will even before we know what it is. Knowing that whatever He asks us to do, He will give us the grace to do it. Then and only then will we be able to stand tall and say,

> **"I can do all things through Him who strengthens me."** (Philippians 4:13 NIV)

Any time we are committed to doing something for God and obeying His will, Satan will do his best to try to get us off course. We must learn to be sensitive to the leading of the Holy Spirit, in order to discern what is from God and what is placed before us to lead us down a wrong path.

> **Do not follow the crowd in doing wrong.** (Exodus 23:2 NIV)

Just because others may do things a certain way doesn't mean you should follow along. Ask God for guidance so that you will stay on the right track. And trust that guidance to lead you in the right direction, even if it doesn't make sense to you right away.

"Commit your way to the Lord; trust in Him." (Psalm 37:5 NIV)

Step 2: Building the foundation

To achieve success in anything you must build upon a secure foundation. Spiritual success only comes from securing a firm foundation with the Father. Developing a strong relationship with God is vital in our Christian walk. We can't trust Him if we don't have an intimate relationship with Him. Once we learn to trust Him, then it will be much easier to obey Him. It's in obedience to God's will that we are led to achieve far more than we could ever imagine for ourselves.

An excellent example of this type of trust is in Luke 5:4-7. Jesus told Simon,

> *"Put out into deep water, and let down the nets for a catch." Simon answered, "Master, we've worked hard all night and haven't caught anything. But because you say so, I will let down the nets."*

> *When they had done so, they caught such a large number of fish that their nets began to break. So they signaled their partners in the other boat to come and help them, and they came and filled both boats so full that they began to sink.*

I'm sure you have heard the saying, "God doesn't call the qualified, but He qualifies the called." That is so true. We only need to be a willing vessel and He will use us for His glory. I have often prayed, "Lord search me out and cleanse me so that I will be a vessel worthy of use by you." I know there is nothing I can do on my own to bring God the glory He deserves. But if I allow Him to mold me into the sort of vessel He can use, then He can work through me to achieve the things He desires.

Along the way there will be those who criticize you for the things you do. They will ridicule you and tell you that you're crazy for doing certain things. But God's Word clearly tells us to

"Bless them that curse you, and pray for them who despitefully use you." (Luke 6:28 NIV)

Once we learn to do that, we are far more likely to obey God's voice. There will be times when the enemy will try to convince you that what you are doing, or what you have done already, is not really what God told you to do, but something you wanted to *believe* God told you to do. But God gives us his Holy Spirit to enable us and empower us to carry out the plans He has for our lives. Trust him! Depend on Him completely.

Trust in the Lord with all your heart and lean not on your own understanding; in all your ways submit to Him, and He will make your paths straight. (Proverbs 3:5-6 NIV)

We should put our trust in God rather than in ourselves because, while our human perceptions are subjective, and our understanding small, He sees and understands everything. He can guide us along in life much better than we could ever guide ourselves.

The more time we spend with God, the better we will be able to understand what He is saying to us. Learning to communicate with Him is the best way for us to know His voice.

Ways God speaks to us:

> *Through Scripture*
> *That still, small voice in our heart*
> *His Spirit communes with our spirit*
> *He will speak through others*
> *Bringing something to our remembrance in a time of need*

But always remember, if what you are "hearing" doesn't line up with His word, it isn't God speaking. God will reveal His thoughts to us in such a way that we can be certain it is from Him.

> **He who forms the mountains, creates the wind, and reveals His thoughts to man, He who turns dawn to darkness, and treads the high places of the earth – the Lord God Almighty is His name.** (Amos 4:13 NIV)

He loves us and wants to have a relationship with us that will allow Him to communicate with us and tell us amazing things.

> *"Call to me, and I will answer you, and show you great and mighty things, which you do not know"* (Jeremiah 33:3 NIV)

If it's knowledge you want, there is no better place to go than to the One who knows EVERYTHING.

> *Oh the depth of the riches of the wisdom and knowledge of God!* (Romans 11:33 NIV)

Step 3: Timing is everything

Now that you have made the commitment and laid the foundation, you may think you are ready to jump right in and start conquering the world for Jesus. You've done the ground work and now you are ready to get this thing going, right? But as the Bible teaches us, there is a time and place for everything. Just keep in mind that things may not happen as quickly as you think they should. We must wait upon the Lord for direction, and do things when He says the time is right. God's timing is perfect. But God's time is not our time, so often we must wait.

Waiting is sometimes the hardest part.

"But they that wait upon the Lord shall renew their strength; they shall mount up with wings as eagles; they shall run, and not be weary; and they shall walk, and not faint." (Isaiah 40:31 NIV)

You may feel that you are just sitting around twiddling your thumbs waiting for an opportunity to prove you can do this. Be patient. God will lead you into the perfect situation when the time is right. But you must trust that God knows what He is doing. He can see the big picture, while we see only what is currently in front of us. That is when we must

Be still and know that He is God. (Psalm 46:10 NIV)

He will orchestrate a divine appointment, a place and time when just the right circumstances are in line for you to intercept with the very person who needs to hear what God wants you to share with them. Recognize that these times are not by accident.

When the time comes, and God leads you into a situation where He wants you to do a work for Him, you must listen and obey. Isaiah 8:9 tells us,

God's ways are not our ways.

Sometimes God's ways may seem utterly outrageous to us, but we have to remember, they are always better, because God's plan is far more than we can see or know. Every unexpected event and delay is for a reason. These are the times when God wants us to learn to trust first and understand later. If you jump ahead instead of waiting for guidance from God, you may find yourself in a jam real quick.

God wants you to be successful in the things He gives you to do, so listen to Him. Do things exactly the way He tells you to, and then it will turn out much better than you could ever imagine. The plans God has for you are far greater than those you have planned for yourself! Trust His timing, not your own.

Step 4: Testing / Quality Assurance

Because we are human, there will be times when we are tempted to do things our own way. In fact, there will be a lot of those times. We tend to think that we have to be completely logical about the way we do things, and face it, God's way doesn't always appear very logical to us. But instead of using logic alone, God wants us to practice using our faith as well. It's in those times that we will be tested. Are you going to do it the logical way, or trust that God is leading you in a better way?

Think about the time when Jesus was washing the disciple's feet. Do you remember what happened when it was time for Him to wash Peter's feet? Peter wholeheartedly objected. He was not about to let the Messiah do something so degrading as washing his nasty feet. But Jesus told him,

"What I am doing you do not understand now, but afterward you will understand."

He had to trust that Jesus knew what He was doing. And you must do the same. You have to trust in the Lord with all your heart... and lean not on your own understanding.

The times of testing will build your faith and endurance.

"... the testing of your faith develops perseverance. Perseverance must finish its work so that you may be mature and complete, not lacking anything." (James 1:3-4 NIV)

Endurance is another thing we desperately need in our Christian walk. We must learn to persevere through the hard times that are bound to come. Jesus has clearly told us,

"In this world you will have trouble. But take heart! I have overcome the world." (John 16:33 NIV)

Sometimes God allows us to go through troubled times so He can teach us something we really need to learn. I went through such a time several years ago. I had just started a new job and was very excited about this new opportunity. At the interview it seemed the boss and I would get along great. However, after a couple of months that proved to be quite the opposite.

As it turned out, she was a woman with an attitude on a power trip. I have never been one to go out of my way to try to "impress the powers that be" and I wasn't about to start with her. I have always been a very hard worker and felt that my work ethic should speak for itself where bosses were concerned. Many of my co-workers didn't feel that way though. They would go way out of their way to do things to earn the extra brownie points. Eventually the boss lady decided she didn't like me and she was determined to make an example of me.

She loved to embarrass me in front of the other employees. She enjoyed yelling at me and then laughing about it with my co-workers. For a while I tried being the better person and just let it ride, but it soon got to the point where I could no longer do that. The resentment I was feeling for her was festering inside of me. I began to be unchristian-like and would point out things she was doing to me to some of my closest acquaintances there in the office. Of course it didn't help when my "friends" started telling me that I shouldn't let her get away with those things. It made me feel that I was in the right to harbor such spite toward her.

But I knew in my heart that was not the way God wanted me to react. As Christians we are supposed to be willing to turn the other cheek. Although, it felt more right to listen to the devil when he would tell me I was justified in the way I was feeling. But I wasn't justified. God's Word tells us to love our enemies and pray for those who persecute us. Oh I prayed alright, but my prayer was that she would stop being so hateful to me. And there were probably times when I prayed that she would get what she justly deserved. But the months rocked on and she didn't let up. Finally, it got to the point where the stress of it all was making me physically ill. I knew I had to do something, so I decided the best thing I could do was look for another job.

I applied for job after job with no response from any of them. I couldn't understand. I had never really had a problem finding a job before but now it seemed that no one wanted me. Month after month I would think, *"Surely something will come along and I can escape this woman."* I prayed for a new job and I prayed for her to get off my back, but nothing was happening. In fact, things got progressively worse.

Eventually, I realized I couldn't take it anymore. I had endured over two years of torture from this evil and spiteful woman. I was going to quit this job, with or without another one. I knew it was going to be tough financially, but I had to do something NOW. I asked God to please show me what to do. I was willing to do any kind of job to get away from my current situation.

God speaks to me best through His Word, so I sat down and started reading my Bible. I don't remember if I was in that particular chapter with my daily devotionals, or if I just opened it up and started reading, but I found myself in the sixteenth chapter of Genesis. I was reading about Hagar, and when I got to verse nine the words just jumped out at me.

"Go back to your mistress and submit to her."

WHAT? NOOO WAY!!! I can't do that! There is no way I can do that!! Surely God didn't understand the predicament I was in. The woman was downright mean! She would laugh in my face! And although I'm not normally a violent person, I just knew I would lose my temper and end up doing something horrible to her.

Then I thought about a small plaque my mother used to have hanging on a wall at her house. It said, "The will of God will never lead you where the grace of God cannot keep you." And there was a little verse from 1 Corinthians 10:13 that stated,

> *"When you are tempted, He will show you a way out so you can endure."*

The next morning I took a deep breath and went back to work. I knew I was in that particular place at that particular time for a reason. I didn't know what that reason was, and I may never fully know, but God knew. And I had to trust Him. I focused on doing my job and just getting through the day. The issues with my boss never got any better but God gave me the grace to get through it. Just a few weeks later I was told about a job opening with a different company. I applied for the job and they called me for an interview. When it came time to discuss salary I was willing to take whatever I could get, even if it meant a cut in pay. As it turned out, they offered me more than I was currently making.

Today I am still with the same organization and have received excellent raises and two promotions. I love my job and I work with some of the best people in the world. But most importantly, I have a closer relationship with my heavenly Father. All because God gave me the grace to submit to what I perceived an impossible situation. It was definitely something I didn't want to do, and certainly something I would never have been able to accomplish on my own. But His grace was sufficient. He gave me the courage to be humble. And I survived it. God is so incredibly awesome!!!

Everyone in this world has troubles, Christians and non-Christians alike. But as Christians, we have Jesus, who has overcome the world! As long as we are in this world there will always be battles to face. We have to be determined to face those battles head-on and be victorious. We must put on the full armor of God and keep on marching!

"For our struggle is not against flesh and blood, but against the rulers, against the authorities, against the powers of this dark world and against the spiritual forces of evil in the heavenly realms. Therefore put on the full armor of God, so that when the day of evil comes, you may be able to stand your ground..." (Ephesians 6:12 NIV)

We have the assurance that God is on our side, and He has promised He will never leave us or forsake us. In Him we will overcome! God is faithful to His promises. So we must be faithful to Him. There will be many times when we have to go through difficult situations. But through the grace of God, we will not be overcome by them. Hold tightly to that promise and never let go! For it's in the letting go that we begin to sink.

We must NEVER think that our way is better than God's way.

Many are the plans in a man's heart, but it is the Lord's purpose that prevails. (Proverbs 19:21 NIV)

Only He knows what the future holds. We have to submit to Him and accept His way as the only way. Then, and only then, will we be able to stand up under the hardships that come our way.

"Humble yourselves, therefore, under God's mighty hand, that he may lift you up in due time. Cast all your anxiety on him because he cares for you. Be self-controlled and alert. Your enemy the devil prowls around like a roaring lion looking for someone to devour. Resist him, standing firm in the faith, because you know that your brothers throughout the world are undergoing the same kind of sufferings." (1 Peter 5:6-9 NIV)

Step 5: Achieving Success

So how do we achieve true spiritual success? In a nutshell, we can't. Only God can give us such successes. Certainly we must do the things God requires of us, but spiritual success is not something we can earn. It is a gift that our Heavenly Father bestows upon us.

"Not by might nor by power, but by my Spirit," says the Lord Almighty. (Zechariah 4:6 NIV)

God rewards the faithful. When we obey God's will, and submit everything we have, everything we are, and everything we want to His will and not our own, then we will be more successful than we could ever have dreamed possible. Focus your eyes on winning the prize spoken of in Philippians 3:13-14.

Know in your heart that all things work to the good for those who love the Lord and do His will. God will never call you into something and then leave you. He will always be there to help you through whatever circumstance may arise. He doesn't "send" us into situations; He calls us to go with Him. We can count on Him to be with us all the way. We have His word on that. He will be with us to guide and protect us through it all. He wants us to succeed! So we can say with confidence,

"If God is for us, who can be against us?" (Romans 8:31 NIV)

As long as we are willing to submit to Him and obey what He tells us, then He will actually pave the way for us.

> *"See, I am sending an angel ahead of you to guard you along the way and to bring you to the place I have prepared. Pay attention to him and listen to what he says." "If you listen carefully to what he says and do all that I say, I will be an enemy to your enemies and will oppose those who oppose you."* (Exodus 23:20-22 NIV)

Having those promises from the One and Only True God, how could we possibly fail? Yes, there will be times when our faith is tested. There may be some really hard times when we want to throw up our hands and quit. But we have to trust that God knows what He is doing, even when we don't. Then we have to just keep on keepin' on. Because we know,

> *"we are more than conquerors through Him who loved us."* (Romans 8:17 NIV)

Step 6: The Bridge that holds it all together

Once God has blessed you with any type of success, you must be very careful to remember that it was not by your own doing. Many have fallen into the trap of thinking they "deserve" to be successful. We must never forget that our blessings are from God.

"A person can receive only what is given them from heaven" (John 3:27 NIV)

Everything we have belongs to God. It is not ours to do with as we please. We must be good stewards of the things we have been blessed with. We must use that which God has given to us in a manner pleasing to Him. To whom much is given, much is required. The Bible teaches us to give to God's house first, before thinking of your own. The way I see it, it is far more imperative for the gospel to be shared than to increase your personal status.

It is very easy to think you should be able to use the money you make and the time you have for yourself, but if we want to continue to be blessed, then we must be willing to give what we have back to God. That is when we will truly be blessed.

God commands us to give back to Him one tenth of our blessings. I know from experience that when you first start thinking about tithing a tenth of your income it can be a hard thing to do. Most of us work very hard for what we make, so when it comes time to sit down and pay the bills we can get a little stingy thinking about giving any of it away. However, we have to remember that we wouldn't even have an income if God hadn't blessed us with the job we have. When you refuse to give back to God a tenth of what He has blessed you with,

"You earn wages only to put them in a purse with holes in it." (Haggai 1:6 NIV)

You will never be able to see where the money goes. You may pay your bills and buy food and clothes, but you will never get ahead. You will work yourself into the grave and never be able to feel the blessings that will be your reward for giving back to God.

God goes so far as to tell us to test Him in this and see what the outcome will be.

"Bring the whole tithe into the storehouse, that there may be food in my house. Test me in this," says the Lord Almighty, *"and see if I will not throw open the floodgates of heaven and pour out so much blessing that you will not have room enough for it."* (Malachi 3:10 NIV)

Luke 6:38 tells us,

"Give, and it will be given to you. Good measure, pressed down, shaken together, running over, will be put into your lap. For with the measure you use it will be measured back to you."

Now, I know what you're thinking. There are plenty of people out there who do not give anything to God, and they are still wealthy. But that is only temporary wealth.

"Surely the day is coming; it will burn like a furnace. All the arrogant and evildoers will be stubble, and that day that is coming will set them on fire," says the Lord Almighty. "Not a root or a branch will be left to them. But for you who revere my name, the sun of righteousness will rise with healing in its wings. Then you will trample down the wicked; they will be ashes under the soles of your feet on the day when I do these things," says the Lord Almighty. (Malachi 4:1-2 NIV)

We can hoard what we have and then one day die and leave it for someone else to enjoy; or we can use our blessings to bless others. We can selfishly squander our blessings on things we think will bring us happiness, but true happiness will never be bought.

One gives freely, yet grows all the richer; another withholds unduly, but comes to poverty. (Proverbs 11:24 NIV)

Jesus tells us,

"Watch out! Be on your guard against all kinds of greed; a man's life does not consist in the abundance of his possessions." (Luke 12:15 NIV)

No matter what anyone around us does, we must obey God and give back to Him what is justly His. As Jim Elliot said, "He is no fool who gives what he cannot keep to gain that which he cannot lose." But when we give,

"Each of you should give what you have decided in your heart to give, not reluctantly or under compulsion, for God loves a cheerful giver." (2 Corinthians 9:7 NIV)

The blessings we receive from God are meant to be shared. Blessings are like dessert, right? Imagine you have a big beautiful, delicious cake. If you wish, you can sit down and eat the entire thing all by yourself. It will be soooo good when you first start eating it, but after a while you aren't going to feel very well. Or, you could take that cake and share it with some friends. You won't get to eat as much of it (and make yourself sick), but you will certainly enjoy it more with the company of those you are sharing it with. Then, not only you are blessed, but others are blessed as well.

Always remember, when we share our blessings with others we will never have to worry about being in need.

"God will meet all your needs according to His glorious riches in Christ Jesus. (Philippians 4:19 NIV)

Sharing your blessings with others also gives you an awesome opportunity to tell them how good God has been to you. Let your light shine so that others will know what a wonderful God we serve! Matthew 5:16 tells us, *"let your light shine before others, that they may see your good deeds and glorify your Father in heaven."*

So come on! Let's go let our little lights shine like there's no tomorrow!!!

Heed the **Warning**. Don't **Gamble** with your eternity, but **Step into Success**.